NATURE'S FROLIC HOUR: APPRECIATING LAKE GEORGE

A gift with the Lake George Association's appreciation for your generous support on the occasion of our 120th Anniversary.

120
YEARS PROTECTING LAKE GEORGE

Lake George Association, Inc.

Virginia Westbrook

NATURE'S FROLIC HOUR
Appreciating Lake George

by VIRGINIA WESTBROOK

Crown Point, New York | Lakes to Locks Passage, Inc. 2005

Funding for the development of this publication has been provided by Empire State Development as part of Governor George E. Pataki's Lake Champlain/Lake George Waterfront Revitalization Initiative, and the Federal Highway Administration's National Scenic Byway Program through the New York State Department of Transportation, Warren County Planning Department and Lakes to Locks Passage, Inc.

Special thanks to members of the advisory committee who helped shape this guidebook: Tony Hall, Editor and Publisher of the *Lake George Mirror*, Pamela Morin, Warren County Tourism, Dr. Marilyn Van Dyke, Director of Warren County Historical Society and Queensbury Town Historian and Tim Weidner, Director, Chapman Historical Museum, who volunteered many hours scanning the illustrations. Thanks also to the librarians, historians and curators who helped to tease out the special stories nestled in their collections: Todd de Garmo and Albert Fowler, Crandall Library Center for Folklife, History and Cultural Programs in Glens Falls; Margaret Edwards, Lake George Town and Village Historian; Marie Ellsworth, Caldwell-Lake George Library; Maggie McClure, Lake George Historical Association in Lake George Village; Jane O'Connell, Hillview Free Library in Diamond Point; Erin Budis-Coe, The Hyde Collection in Glens Falls and Gerald Pepper, Laura Rice and Angela Donnelly, Adirondack Museum in Blue Mountain Lake. Warm appreciation goes to Julia Corscaden Beaty for sharing her memories of summers spent in Hague and on the waters of Lake George.

FRONT COVER: *Lake George*, by William Hart (American, 1823–1894), oil on canvas c. 1875. Gift of Joseph Jeffers Dodge courtesy of The Hyde Collection, Glens Falls, New York. Photograph by Stephen Sloman © 1999.

BACK COVER: Lake George photograph by Richard K. Dean courtesy of Dean's Distinctive Photography and Dean Color, Glens Falls, New York.

INSIDE COVERS: Lakes to Locks Passage overview map and Lake George Region map developed by Shannon-Rose Design, Saratoga Springs, New York.

PAGE 1: Temple Knoll Island from Island Harbor House, c. 1920 (West Historical Museum, Hague)

TITLE PAGE: Steamboat Landing at Black Mountain Point by S. R. Stoddard, 1880 (Hillview Free Library, Diamond Point)

COPY EDITING: Marie Ellsworth and Tony and Lisa Hall.

ISBN 0-9678366-1-1

Library of Congress Control number: 2005902544

This book is printed on New Leaf Reincarnation Matte 80# text, a recycled and chlorine-free sheet. The typeface used throughout is Scala with Scala Sans. The binding is smyth-sewn. Printed and bound by Friesens, Manitoba, Canada. Design by Christopher Kuntze.

For more detailed directions to sites described in this book, consult the free Lakes to Locks Passage Lake George Region brochure available at visitor information centers, or visit www.lakestolocks.com

LGA
P. O. Box 408
Lake George, NY 12845

PRST STD
US POSTAGE
PAID
GLENS FALLS
PERMIT 511

AMERICA'S OLDEST SUMMER NEWSPAPER

Lake George Mirror

Established 1880

DEVOTED TO THE INTERESTS OF THE QUEEN OF AMERICAN LAKES

July 8, 2005

Lakes to Locks Passage Publishes New Guide to Lake George Communities

By Mirror Staff

First came the interpretive signs. Then a grant to build a Visitors Center in Lake George Village. Now the state and federal funding that created the Lakes to Locks Passage incorporating scenic and historic byways from Albany to the Canadian border has produced a guidebook specifically for the Passage's Lake George loop.

"Nature's Frolic Hour: Appreciating Lake George," a 64 page, illustrated introduction to the region, written by the Crown Point-based historian Virginia Westbrook, was published in late June and will soon be available at museums, bookstores and gift shops throughout the area. The book is not a conventional tourists' handbook listing lodgings, restaurants and a few points of interest; rather, it elaborates upon the theme of the Lakes to Locks Passage, which is that each region is composed of "lives" or layers of history and meaning. In the case of the Lake George region, those layers of history are the natural, the military and the social. The book, which has chapters devoted to all three, corresponds to the interpretive signs installed in

Nature's Frolic Hour: Appreciating Lake George

BY VIRGINIA WESTBROOK

The cover of Lake George's new guidebook features The Hyde's 19th century painting of Lake George, 'Lake George' by William Hart.

the lakeshore communities two summers ago and which help guide visitors interested in one or all three "lives" as they thread their way through upstate New York along the highways of the Lakes to Lock Passage.

Westbrook's book also includes a "gazeteer" for every lake shore community, providing information about the towns' histories, their museums and historic sites and recreational offerings.

Illustrations were provided by the towns' museums and historical societies and feature the work of noted photographers like Seneca Ray Stoddard, Fred Thatcher and Dick Dean.

An advisory committee assembled by Westbrook and consisting of local historians and museum curators assisted the author in the early stages of the work.

Contents

Lake George, N. Y. by Thomas Cole, 1834 (Adirondack Museum, Blue Mountain Lake)

Appreciating Lake George

For generations, Lake George has inspired travelers, authors and artists to try their hand at capturing Nature's glories in words and pictures. Their works offer many windows through which to gaze and wonder at how powerfully scenery can stir the soul.

Appreciation of natural beauty has evolved over the centuries. Soldiers and explorers said little about the beauty of the mountains and waters beyond a brief "romantic view" or "pleasing prospect." They saw Lake George as a stretch of water that could carry them and their gear through miles of wilderness. Only after warfare waned, and the Age of Reason gave way to Romanticism at the end of the eighteenth century, did people begin to acknowledge and explore the feelings that the wonders of nature aroused in them.

Nowhere did this new awareness of aesthetics thrive more than at Lake George. The great landscape artist, Thomas Cole chose this "Holy Lake" as the primier example of beauty in his "Essay on American Scenery," written in 1835, saying that, *the innumerable islets . . . seem to have been sprinkled over the smiling deep in Nature's frolic hour.*

Although Cole lamented the lack of appreciation Americans had for their scenery at the time, his paintings, and those of hundreds of other artists, triggered a rush of travel that grew quickly into a major tourist industry. Those tourists, in turn, supported the artists by buying their paintings, prints and engravings of the places they had visited.

For early tourists with a religious perspective, the evidence of the Creator visible in the

Horicon Sketching Club by S. R. Stoddard, 1882 (Hillview Free Library)

Black Mountain Point by S. R. Stoddard, c. 1875 (Chapman Historical Museum, Glens Falls)

wilderness fulfilled their expectations for grandeur. Only later did people realize the healthful benefits of the outdoors. However, savvy writers promptly realized that understanding enhances appreciation. Guidebooks told the stirring stories of wilderness scouts, sieges and battles, even as they helped readers select the perfect hotel for their holiday and make the rail and steamboat connections to get there.

Today, websites and tourism offices help visitors find their way. Historic sites, museums and wayside exhibits tell the stories. This little book aims to offer enough history to help readers appreciate the many layers of meaning embedded in this spectacular landscape.

Further Reading

More books about Lake George are available now than ever before. Most local libraries feature an "Adirondack" section filled with nature guides, local histories and reminiscences. The following books contributed significantly to the preparation of this guidebook.

Russell P. Bellico's *Sails and Steam in the Mountains: A Maritime and Military History of Lake George and Lake Champlain* (Purple Mountain Press, Revised Edition 2001) delves deeply into the details of three wars fought on the northern lakes. In *Chronicles of Lake George: Journeys in War and Peace* (Purple Mountain Press, 1999), Mr. Bellico annotates first-person accounts of travelers and their guides from Peter Kalm in 1749 to Seneca Ray Stoddard's final 1914 publication.

Many local authors explore the foundations of the tourism business. Betty Ahearn Buckell expanded on her family's experiences in *Old Lake George Hotels* and *Lake George Boats* (Buckle Press). William P. Gates digs into both family and personal history in his *History of the Sagamore Hotel, Lake George Boats and Steamboats* and *History of the Fort William Henry Hotel*. Kathryn E. O'Brien reveals the glittering lifestyle of wealthy summer people in *The Great and the Gracious on Millionaire's Row: Lake George in its Glory*. Theodore Corbett's *The Making of American Resorts* (Rutgers University Press, 2001) examines Lake George in the context of nearby Ballston Spa and Saratoga Springs. Dorothy W. Goodfellow's *Growing Up Wild* (Boxwood Press, 1977) carries a reader back to the isolated life of early 20th-century families dependent on the lake for transporta-

Nellie's Continental Restaurant, c. 1955 (Lake George Village Historian)

tion. Three histories of Silver Bay, two about Glenburnie and Betty Buckell's *No Dull Days at Hulett's* tell the story of "intimate communities". Gale J. Halm and Mary H. Sharp assemble the best images of Lake George in their photographic history, *Lake George* (Arcadia, 2000).

Area museums have made the works of artists in their collections available in lively publications. The Chapman Museum reprinted Seneca Ray Stoddard's original 1874 guidebook, *The Adirondacks Illustrated*, in 1983. The Adirondack Museum makes scholarly sense out of the myriad images of the region in *Wild Impressions: the Adirondacks on Paper* (1995) by Georgia B. Barnhill and *Adirondack Prints and Printmakers* edited by Caroline Welsh (1998). This publication coincides with the opening of a comprehensive exhibition with an accompanying catalogue, *Painting Lake George, 1774-1900* at The Hyde Collection in Glens Falls.

Lay of the Land

Nature's forces have sculpted an extraordinary landscape around Lake George. Underneath the lake, and the forested hillsides that enfold it, lies some of the most ancient rock in the world, formed more than a billion years ago when Africa collided with North America. The tectonic impact folded up layers of sea floor and squeezed them together deep in the earth where they mixed with molten magma and slowly cooled into hard, crystalline rock.

This ancestral core of the Adirondacks lay buried for another 500 million years as deposits settled onto yet another ocean floor, forming layers of sandstone and limestone. Then, the mass of rock cracked into huge blocks. Some of the blocks dropped while others rose, in a process now called "block faulting." The up-thrust blocks became mountains; the dropped blocks now form the bottom of Lake George.

Caldwell by William Henry Bartlett, 1840 (author's collection)

The Narrows, pitch pine detail, by John Henry Hill, 1871
(Adirondack Museum, Blue Mountain Lake)

Summit of Rogers Rock looking north, 2004 (Lake George Land Conservancy,
Bolton Landing)

Map of Lake Champlain and Lake George, southern river outlet detail, by S.R. Stoddard,
1892 (author's collection)

One Lake from Two River Valleys

Before the last Ice Age began, the lakebed consisted of two separate valleys whose rivers flowed in opposite directions. One stream rose to the west of Tongue Mountain and flowed southeast, around the east flank of French Mountain. The other drained north, skirting the west side of Rogers Rock to reach the Trout Brook valley in Ticonderoga.

The power of moving ice revised that landscape. Beginning about 1.5 million years ago, a continental ice sheet crept down from the north. The ice eventually built up to a mile thick. It expanded in lobes, or streams, that gouged out valleys and scraped over mountains. Only the hardest rock could resist the slow, crunching motion of the glacier. Softer rocks, including most of the limestone and sandstone deposits, were swept up, adding grit to the ice and helping to scrape away everything that would move.

When the climate warmed and the glacier began to melt, all the soil and rock in the ice fell to the ground. Tons of material dropped right into the river courses, effectively damming them up. Water filled the new lake until it found an outlet over the natural dam at the north end of the valley.

"Indian Kettles" on the western shore of the lake give an indication of the power of glacial melt water. These perfectly circular holes in granite bedrock got their name from the romantic notion that Indians carved them as

Natural dam at Lake George outlet by Elara Tanguy, 2005

Indian Kettles c. 1920 (West Historical Museum, Hague)

The shores of Lake George evoked "emotions approximating rapture," in the words of Reverend Timothy Dwight in 1802. The rocky terrain, topped with a jumble of jagged trees, embodied the very essence of the picturesque wilderness. The random scattering of so many "tufted" islands enhanced the scenery further, especially when smooth water doubled their beauty in reflection.

Lake George State Campgrounds
Anyone can camp on the shores of Lake George thanks to the efforts of a handful of conservation-minded outdoorsmen who fought the battles necessary to bring two thirds of Lake George's 162 islands under State ownership. The New York State Department of Environmental Conservation (NYS DEC) maintains campsites on many of the islands and on Hearthstone and Black Mountain Points.

cooking pots. Instead, they were carved by small stones caught in a whirlpool long enough to bore holes nearly six feet deep.

Picturesque Shores

The pristine clarity of Lake George water stands out as the defining feature of this place. Underwater cliffs, boulders and shoals can be as captivating as the view above the surface of the lake, especially if you can spot fish in the depths. Such clear water comes from underground springs and the contents of short streams that carry very little grit into the lake. Underwater meadows help filter the water further. A thin layer of glacial till makes up the meager soil.

The Narrows by William Henry Bartlett, 1840 (author's collection)

Weliket Camp, c.1920 (Lake George Historical Association)

Inspiring Prospects

Mountains that rise a thousand feet or more above the surface of Lake George offer grand prospects for anyone willing to climb the slopes. In many places, trees have not yet taken hold, so nothing blocks the view. Most of the land is preserved by New York State as part of the Adirondack Forest Preserve.

On the eastern shore, the trails follow old carriage roads and bridle paths. Switchbacks and bridges make the going much easier on these trails than on the mountains to the west. A network of paths link the summits with seven sylvan ponds whose surrounding stands of maple make them particularly spectacular in autumn.

The maze of interconnecting trails can be very confusing without a detailed trail guide. The Adirondack Mountain Club publishes a series of trail guides to all of the Adirondacks. Lake George Land Conservancy publishes maps for trails on their protected lands. NYS DEC has trail maps for State lands.

Prospect Mountain

As the mountain nearest to Lake George Village, Prospect Mountain attracts immediate attention, but the hiking trail is most appropriate for young scouts. The first stretch involves climbing stairs and crossing a bridge over the highway. After that, the trail follows the roadbed of the old inclined railway straight up the mountain. The faint of heart might better pay the day-use fee and drive up Veterans Memorial Highway or take the DEC Shuttle from the parking lot to the summit.

The Narrows, island detail, by John Henry Hill, 1871 (Adirondack Museum, Blue Mountain Lake)

Black Mountain, S. R. Stoddard c. 1880 (Chapman Historical Museum, Glens Falls)

Upper Cascade of Shelving Rock Falls by John Henry Hill, 1871 (Adirondack Museum, Blue Mountain Lake)

Cat and Thomas Mountains

A Lake George Land Conservancy Preserve protects the Edgecomb Pond watershed west of Bolton Landing. Seven miles of trails to the summits reward hikers with outstanding views of Lake George's south and central basins. The Conservancy publishes a trail guide to the Preserve.

Tongue Mountain

This twelve-mile spur of a mountain divides Northwest Bay from the Narrows, affording spectacular views from any of six peaks along its spine. Two trail heads on Route 9N lead to 20 miles of trail criss-crossing the mountain. A NYS DEC "car top" boat launch on Northwest Brook gives access to the bay and Montcalm

Climber on Rogers Slide, 2004 (Adirondack Rock and River, Keene)

Shelving Rock Mountain by S.R. Stoddard c.1875 (Caldwell-Lake George Library, Lake George Village)

Point without making the grueling 25-mile round trip.

Rogers Rock

A trail up the back side of Rogers Rock starts at campsite # 184 in Rogers Rock State Campground. The half-mile ascent feels almost as steep as the "slide," which is a great favorite with rock climbers. The trail continues another half mile through oak and white pine woods before opening up to the lake view made famous by the legend of Robert Rogers' escape after the Battle on Snowshoes in 1757.

Cook Mountain

The Lake George Land Conservancy maintains the Cook Mountain Preserve, located on Baldwin Road in Ticonderoga. A short, steep hike leads to a southerly view of the lake from the summit where scrub-oaks and blueberries cling to bare granite.

Black Mountain

Black Mountain rises several hundred feet above its neighbors. Its commanding summit can be reached by a 3-mile trail rising 2300 feet up from Black Mountain Point on the lake shore, or by a 2.5-mile trail from Pike Brook Road that climbs only half that distance. The broad lake spreads out below, but the west shoulder of the mountain blocks a view of The Narrows.

Sleeping Beauty Mountain

A loop trail follows a well-constructed road with switchbacks that ease the climb to the dramatic cliffs at the top of Sleeping Beauty Mountain. Ledges just below the summit offer views to the south and west, as well as to the north. Along the way, another trail leads to Erebus Mountain, but there is no view from the summit.

Shelving Rock Mountain & Falls

A gentle climb for a mile and a half along a horse trail leads you to the overgrown summit of Shelving Rock Mountain, but overlooks open up along the way. Shelving Rock Falls lies nestled at the heart of a maze of streams and trails.

Buck Mountain

Two trails approach Buck Mountain from opposite directions. The one from the east is not as steep and substitutes a beaver pond and a cascade for the vistas available from the trail skirting the shoulder of Pilot Knob. From the rocky summit, you can look down on all the peaks this side of Black Mountain.

Pilot Knob Ridge

A two-mile hiking loop through the Lake George Land Conservancy's Pilot Knob Ridge Preserve skirts patches of jack-in-the-pulpit and pink lady's slipper on the way to panoramic views of the entire south basin and southern Adirondacks in the distance.

Heron Rookery by Elara Tanguy, 2005

Heron live in the most uncomfortable looking places. Nests of large sticks loom eerily in the skeletons of dead trees. Gull Bay Preserve protects a heron rookery in an abandoned beaver pond near Gull Bay. They can also be seen feeding in the slack water behind Million Dollar Beach.

Places for People

Only a few places on Lake George offered a foothold for habitation. The beach at the head of the lake, Assembly and Ripley Points, Shelving Rock, Sabbath Day Point: none of them fit for growing much, but just right for a group of Indian families to spend the summer hunting, fishing, and gathering the fruits of the land.

Evidence buried in the thin, shaggy layer of soil tells us that people have come to the shores of Lake George to gather nature's bounty for a very long time. Fireplace charcoal found at

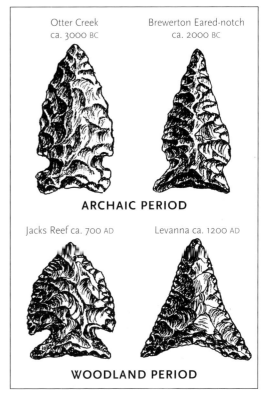

Projectile points typical of the Lake George basin by Frank Schlamp, 2005

Native American statue in Lake George Battlefield Park by A.P. Proctor, 1919 (Lake George Village Historian)

Sabbath Day Point by S.R. Stoddard, c. 1880 (Chapman Historical Museum, Glens Falls)

Harris Bay dates back 6000 years. Early Indian people left behind carefully-shaped stone points used for hunting. Pottery shards indicate that more recent Woodland people also spent time on the lakeshore.

The historical record tells us too little about the Indian presence in this valley, but the glimpses that survive suggest that the Indians never went very far away. They practiced the hunter's art of being invisible in plain sight, emerging from their camouflage only when it suited them.

According to Indian tradition, Mitchell Sabbatis (pronounced "Sabbatay") presided over a summer village on the sandy point just north of The Narrows. There, the Indians extended friendly hospitality to mid-18th-century travelers. At the end of the French and Indian War the land was granted to Samuel Adams, who opened a tavern. Just three years after the close of the Revolutionary War, the name of the place had already been corrupted to "Sabbath Day" Point.

Risky Lives

The arrival of Europeans in the 17th century turned the Lake George region into a dangerous place. French explorers and missionaries, Dutch traders as well as soldiers and settlers disturbed the balance of life among the Indians, who had shared the valley as a pathway for travel and a seasonal hunting ground. France and Britain both wanted to own the country and they were prepared to fight each other for it. After the armies dispersed, settlers who expected to make their living at farming found their livelihood still at risk.

A Warriors' Wilderness

Struggle for control of North America took the form of raids launched by one side or the other during three colonial wars, which we call by the names of the British monarch of the time: King William's War (1689–1697), Queen Anne's War (1702–1713) and King George's War (1744–1748). Many of the raiding parties traveled Lake George to reach their quarry.

Colonial warfare came to a head in the Seven Years War, known in America as the French and Indian War because the French

A Prospective view of the battle fought Near Lake George, Bloody Morning Scout detail, by Samuel Blodget, 1756 (Fort Ticonderoga)

Launch of Abercromby's army, July 1758 by Frederick C. Yohn, c. 1910 (Chapman Historical Museum, Glens Falls)

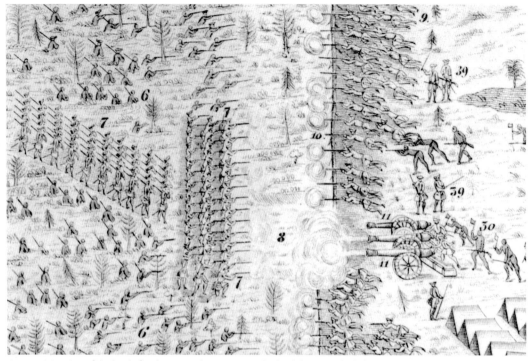

A Prospective view of the battle fought Near Lake George, Battle detail, by Samuel Blodget, 1756 (Fort Ticonderoga)

Williams Monument by S. R. Stoddard, c. 1875 (Chapman Historical Museum, Glens Falls)

Society of Colonial Wars Monument to the Battle of Lake George, 1903 (Lake George Village Historian)

enlisted Indians from as far away as Lake Superior to help them fight the British. From 1755 to 1759, huge armies assembled on the shores of Lake George to fight a series of battles that would determine the fate of North America.

The Battle of Lake George opened the hostilities in 1755, playing out in three stages on the route connecting Lake George with the Hudson River. An engraving of the battle published three months later is the first American image of an historical event. Today, interpretive signs along the Warren County Bicycle Trail identify the spots and explain the complex series of events, including the death of Colonel Ephraim Williams, commanding Massachusetts provincial troops. The terms of his will established Williams College in Williamstown, Massachusetts.

Forts at Lake George

After the battle, General William Johnson ordered his troops to construct defensive breastworks to protect the camp area. Later, Fort William Henry was expanded into a traditional star-shaped fort designed to support a garrison of 500 men. The fort survived the first French assault in the late winter of 1757, but capitulated after several days of siege the following summer.

The British launched two more campaigns against the French. In 1758, General Abercromby's army of 15,000 troops camped all around the place where Fort William Henry had stood the previous year before sailing down the lake to their disastrous defeat at the Heights of Carillon at Ticonderoga. The following year, General Jeffery Amherst ordered construction of a new fort on rising ground to the east. The walls of the new Fort George were to be faced with stone but soldiers completed only one bastion before they were ordered north to begin a new fort at Crown Point on Lake Champlain.

Fort George's earthworks look like grassy mounds today, but statues and interpretive exhibits guide a visitor's ramblings through Lake George Battlefield Park. Since 1953, the reconstruction of Fort William Henry has added a living-history experience to the spectacular view from the ramparts.

Perspective View of Lake George by Captain-Lieutenant Henry Skinner, 1759 (Fort Ticonderoga)

Fort William Henry (Fort William Henry, Lake George Village)

Ruins of Fort George by S. R. Stoddard, c. 1875 (Chapman Historical Museum, Glens Falls)

Revolutionary Times

Fort George fell into American hands within a day or two of the capture of Fort Ticonderoga in May 1775. It served as the main personnel and logistic supply base supporting the Northern Army from 1775–1777.

Henry Knox transported 59 artillery pieces from Fort Ticonderoga across Lake George in the winter of 1775–1776. Orders from General Washington directed Knox to bring the artillery to Massachusetts. Mounted on Dorchester Heights, trained on the British occupation, the captured cannon drove the British out of Boston on March 17, 1776.

Fort George lay in the path of General Burgoyne's army after they had recaptured Fort Ticonderoga. American forces retreated from Fort George in the face of the British invasion, returning after the victory at Saratoga in October 1777. British forces captured and burned Fort George during Carleton's raid in 1780.

Sunken Treasures

Armies used hundreds of boats to transport troops and supplies across Lake George. At the end of the 1758 season, Abercromby's men sank an entire fleet of bateaux, whaleboats, row galleys, a sloop and two radeaux to preserve them for another campaign. One radeau, a huge floating gun platform, slipped irretrievably into deep water. The 52-foot *Land Tortoise* (illus. p.21, left) still lies where it settled.

Several smaller boats escaped notice when Amherst's men returned to retrieve them.

The remains of some of this sunken fleet are now protected as part of a shipwreck park called New York State Submerged Heritage Preserve. A volunteer underwater archaeology group called *Bateaux Below*, which discovered, identified, mapped and helped preserve many wrecks, prepared a brochure to help divers explore the underwater preserve.

Francis Parkman journeyed down Lake George in the summer of 1842 on a personal odyssey to explore the landscape that shaped the movement of armies during the French and Indian War. What he saw lived on in his mind's eye for a lifetime, supplying the sense of place that gave his many histories of the "old French War" such vivid life.

Henry Knox marker and cannon, c.1960 (Fort Ticonderoga)

Benjamin Franklin crossing Lake George by bateau en route to Canada in 1776 by Elayne Sears, 2000 (Fort Ticonderoga)

Colonial bateau, a 25-35-foot wooden warship, by Mark Peckham, c.1995 (Bateaux Below, Wilton)

"Living on Fish and Strangers"

This 19th-century quip neatly captures the challenge of life on the shores of Lake George. Benjamin Silliman declared that the land appeared "utterly incapable of cultivation" when he visited in 1819. But that didn't keep people from trying to establish farms on whatever level ground they could find. Sloping ground at Hulett's Bay, Blaire's Bay (opposite Hague) and along Northwest Bay (behind Bolton Landing), supported farming, as did the valley west of Tongue Mountain, known as Wardsboro. With these few exceptions, farming near the lake was limited to hotel kitchen gardens to feed guests.

Town centers grew up around the landing places. Caldwell (renamed Lake George in 1962) commanded the head of the lake, launching and receiving travelers. Bolton began in the shelter of Huddle Bay, but moved north as larger vessels required deeper water to dock. Hague perched at the outlet of a brook that carved a path westward over the mountains. The northern landing at Ticonderoga never assembled a separate population because an early hamlet known as Alexandria developed nearby, where mills clustered around the upper falls of LaChute River (formerly Ticonderoga Creek).

The land between Lake George and the Hudson River proved much more welcoming. A group of Quakers settled comfortably there after the French and Indian War but fled at the outbreak of the Revolution. The next wave of newcomers found that the gently rolling glacial till supported good crops of grain, potatoes and

Hague farm, c. 1910 (West Historical Museum, Hague)

Steve Holman and granddaughter with potato harvest, c. 1910 (West Historical Museum, Hague)

apples. Construction of the Feeder Canal from the Hudson River to Hudson Falls gave farmers an outlet to southern markets. Several beautiful barns survive along Ridge and Bay Roads to pinpoint the most productive farmland in the area.

George Brown gravestone by Elara Tanguy, 2005

Reverend George S. Brown built stone walls when he wasn't busy saving souls. People gathered by the hundreds to hear "The Black Man" preach the message of Methodism in Bolton, Hague, Caldwell, Dunham's Bay, and Queensbury in the 1830s. Later Brown spent several years as a missionary in Liberia, but returned to Glens Falls in his old age.

Weeks' barn, Ridge Road, c. 2000 (Queensbury Town Historian)

Riches in the Mountains

For a place of bounteous beauty, Lake George appeared to offer unlimited commercial opportunities. A blanket of trees kept timber harvesters busy for all of the 19th century. Graphite deposits in the mountains of Hague supported a mining town for half a century. Most of the area's industrial activity focused on Ticonderoga to the north or the Hudson River to the south. Timber and graphite moved down the lake to mills in Ticonderoga. Bolton and Lake George sawed their own lumber. The owners of Hudson River factories built splendid estates on the shores of Lake George for their rest and relaxation.

Getting Around

Oars and sails carried the first passengers up and down the lake. Sails worked only when the wind blew in the right direction, unless you needed them as a tarp to fend off a squall. This happened to young Abigail May who went down the lake to visit the ruins of Fort Ticonderoga in 1800. Four oarsmen rowed the "bark" that carried her and six others. With a stop for dinner and a second to give the men a rest, the trip took all day.

Steamboats soon relieved the oarsmen of their labors. The *Queensbury Packet* was built in Dunham's Bay in 1815. The *James Caldwell* went

Sagamore Dock c. 1910 (Chapman Historical Museum, Glens Falls)

Saloon of steamboat *Minne-Ha-Ha* by S.R. Stoddard, 1880 (Hillview Free Library, Diamond Point)

into service in 1817, though she only sailed two seasons before fire put her out of business. The next boat, *Mountaineer*, built in 1824, began the era of regular service, making intermediate stops at Bolton and Hague. The *William Caldwell*, built at Homelands Dock at the north end of the lake, initiated connecting service by stagecoach through Ticonderoga to the Fort

Ticonderoga landing on Lake Champlain. Her successor, *John Jay*, caught fire and sank near Hague in 1856. Six additional vessels served out the remainder of the century.

After 1871, steamboats on both Lake George and Lake Champlain operated under the control of the Delaware and Hudson Canal Company whose main business was building

railroads. The company built a spur to connect Ticonderoga's Baldwin Dock with a north-south main line on Lake Champlain in 1874. A branch line from Glens Falls replaced the stagecoach service to Caldwell (Lake George) in 1882. The tracks ran right out onto the steamboat dock for easy transfer of passengers and baggage.

Wm. R. Potter,

Advertisement for steam launch, *Olive*, 1894 (Adirondack Museum, Blue Mountain Lake)

Pilot Knob still lives up to the name given to it by the captains of big steamboats in the mid-1800s. Today's captains use Pilot Knob as a heading when they leave Bolton Landing pier to navigate the narrow passage between Gull Rock and Recluse Island. Going north from Lake George Village, steering for Pilot Knob helps them avoid shallow water east of ⁝⁝⁝⁝ ⁝⁝⁝⁝⁝⁝

Horicon docked at Hulett's Landing by S.R. Stoddard, c.1880 (Chapman Historical Museum, Glens Falls)

ber, but most of the harvest from the lake's north basin floated down to the outlet of Lake George where the mills of the Ticonderoga hamlet of Alexandria sawed them into lumber.

Mining Graphite

Up in back of Hague, only a stretch of stone walls wending through the woods, or a sentinel apple tree, give any indication that the hillsides were ever inhabited. No one lived here until the 1880s, when a surveyor located deposits of "black lead" in several lots. A factory for refining this valuable mineral was already running in downtown Ticonderoga. Joseph Dixon Crucible Company moved quickly to establish mining and concentrating works at a place that came to be known, simply, as Graphite.

Graphite mine, c. 1890 (West Historical Museum, Hague)

Lumbering in Winter by Winslow Homer, July 1871 (Adirondack Museum, Blue Mountain Lake)

Cutting Trees

The first "crop" harvested from the Lake George shore was cut in winter, when frozen ground and snow cover made it possible to move logs through the forest. As timber cutters moved further and further into the woods, they lived in logging camps for the entire season, leaving their families to weather the winter on their own.

In contrast, the milling of timber required warmer weather because sawmills ran on waterpower. Three sawmills built in Bolton in 1820 sawed logs stored in a "boom" in Sawmill Bay. A sawmill on Hague Brook cut local tim-

Bolton saw mill, 1909 (Bolton Historical Museum, Bolton Landing)

Miners dug the first shaft in 1887 and erected a crushing mill to concentrate the ore. A rough hamlet with several boarding houses, a tavern and store promptly surrounded the works. Wagons hauled concentrated ore to the lakeshore for shipment to Ticonderoga. They traveled a track so narrow that teamsters had to use a different road on their return trip. Production peaked in 1912 at two and a half million pounds per year. New foreign sources soon undercut the high cost of underground mines in this remote place. The mines at Hague closed on April 1, 1921 but their story can still be found exhibited at the West Historical Museum in the Hague Community Center and at the Ticonderoga Heritage Museum.

Harvesting Ice

The waters of Lake George earned just as high praise frozen as they did in liquid form. Every hotel, and most of the grand summer homes, had an icehouse where blocks of ice were bedded down in an insulating layer of sawdust. In summer, the ice emerged to cool ice boxes, chill summer drinks, or to make ice cream.

Commercial ice harvesters used horse-drawn saws to cut ice from the frozen lake. Then they stacked the blocks of ice in layers of sawdust in large lakeside warehouses. Some Lake George ice was shipped south by rail. The rest was sold to summer customers. The Bolton Historical Museum displays ice cutting equipment used at Sawmill Bay. Johnson Ice Company in Lake George continued cutting ice until the middle of the 20th century. Their machinery is now part of the Washington County Farm Museum at the Fairgrounds in Easton, in the Champlain Canal Region of Lakes to Locks Passage.

Cutting ice at Bolton by Elara Tanguy, 2005

First crushing mill at Graphite, 1888 (West Historical Museum, Hague)

Resorting to Nature

People started coming to Lake George before there were places to accommodate them. Abby May reported in 1800 that the only place in Caldwell big enough to hold her group "did not promise much." When Francis Parkman arrived at Sabbath Day Point in 1842, he settled for "an old, rickety, dingy shingle place with a potato garden in front and hogs perambulating the outhouses."

Civilization quickly caught up with the tourist traffic as farmhouses expanded to take in guests, followed closely by purpose-built hotels that clustered comfortably around the public landings. Steamboats also docked at the private landings of many of these "houses," as they preferred to be called. The heyday of hotels lasted only a few decades, giving way to changing patterns of leisure-time activities.

The 20th century brought changes of ownership that would dramatically transform the landscape. As individuals began to build their own summer homes, the development pattern expanded outwards from clusters of buildings near landings, to a continuous strip along the lakeshore. Even the open space that buffered the mansions of "the great and the gracious"

Canoeists, c. 1920 (Lake George Historical Association)

North terrace, Kattskill House by S.R. Stoddard, c. 1880 (Chapman Historical Museum, Glens Falls)

100-Island House at Fourteen-Mile Island, c.1900 (Adirondack Museum, Blue Mountain Lake)

eventually gave way to rustic camps, vacation cabins and motels.

Loss of the natural shoreline caused a reaction that grew into an environmental movement. A citizens' group dedicated to water quality, a statewide movement for preserving wilderness and a ground swell of interest in public access to nature combined, at Lake George, to achieve groundbreaking work in the conservation of natural resources.

For a hundred years, the Abenaki people had hidden themselves as expertly in the midst of white society as they ever did (and do) in the forest. One exception to Indian invisibility was the summer camp at Lake George, where a group of families assembled to make and sell baskets to tourists. Similar trade took place in other summer resorts, but Lake George is where Seneca Ray Stoddard recorded them through his lens.

Indian basket maker by S.R. Stoddard c. 1880 (Chapman Historical Museum, Glens Falls)

Thrill of the Chase

Folks may grumble that "you can't eat the scenery," but there have always been plenty of edible creatures living within it. Nineteenth-century writers never failed to mention the abundance of fish and game available in and around Lake George. Benjamin Silliman (1819) believed that "nothing of the kind can be finer" than trout from Lake George. Harriet Martineau (1835) observed that the water was clear enough that a fisherman could pick out the particular fish he wanted to catch. Anyone passing time on the lake could count on catching a mid-day dinner and enjoying it around the cooking fire.

Deer lore kept pace with fish stories. A British officer traveling south with General Burgoyne's artillery train first reported on the local custom of hunting deer with packs of dogs that drove deer into the lake where a waiting boatman completed the kill. Rev. Timothy Dwight (1803) wrote at length on the strategy, teamwork and high emotional tension of this manner of chase.

Travelers read about the hunt in guidebooks and admired the vertical prominence named Deer Leap, but these forces of legend could not compete with the power of a picture. William Henry Bartlett added the drama of a deer kill to the foreground of his view of Black Mountain,

Hunting guides Asa & Jim Leach, Bernie Clifton, Cub Miller,1897 (West Historical Museum, Hague)

Black Mountain by William Henry Bartlett, 1840 (author's collection)

Ethel Thompson at Diamond Point, c. 1910 (Lake George Historian)

drawn for *American Scenery* in 1837–1839. This British publication brought the American landscape to the firesides of distant readers.

Hunting and fishing still hold great appeal. Deer season brings hunters to the woods surrounding Lake George. Today, they come armed with more humanitarian weapons and find shelter in the lean-tos built by the New York State DEC. Fall hikers would do well to wear blaze orange to be certain they aren't mistaken for game. Fishing even goes on in winter when the coves and bays freeze over.

Picturing Scenery

The sublime scenery of Lake George moved many an artist to share the experience with the wider world. The first pictures were drawn with words. Travelers' accounts, like that of Timothy Dwight (1802), glowed "with emotions approximating rapture." Long before most books had pictures, the fervor of language sounded a clarion cry: get thee to the wilderness!

Pictures came along very soon. Daniel Wadsworth drew two Lake George views for a book by Benjamin Silliman published in 1820. Thomas Cole made his first trip to Lake George in 1826. He brought his friend, Asher B. Durand, with him on a later visit. These and other talented painters (many encouraged by Wadsworth) captured landscape views on canvas that would later become known as America's first unique artistic style, the Hudson River School of painting.

Printed engravings of artists' work fed an insatiable public appetite for images of this grand, new country. A custom of giving literary

The Road to Lake George by Winslow Homer, July 1869 (Adirondack Museum, Blue Mountain Lake)

"gift books" at New Year's provided an outlet for illustrated travel articles. William Henry Bartlett, sent to America on assignment for a book on American scenery, produced six different views of Lake George that were reprinted many times over.

As better incomes gave people the means to travel, new, illustrated magazines fed their desires. Travel articles enticed them with the glories of nature in language that helped them appreciate what they saw. Winslow Homer's first Adirondack illustration, "The Road to Lake

Tent of Horicon Sketching Club by S.R. Stoddard, 1880 (Hillview Free Library, Diamond Point)

George," published in 1869, showed children waving to a stagecoach loaded with holiday-makers, many of whom came prepared to sketch or paint *en plein air* (outdoors), just as they saw artists doing in the magazines.

Photography created a new set of possibilities, especially when combined with the nearly simultaneous invention of the stereo viewer which gave images realistic depth. Lake George

qualified as an "exotic" location, along with the cathedrals of Europe and views of the Holy Land, as popular subjects of stereo views.

Many photographers made a good living from sales of stereo views, but Seneca Ray Stoddard of Glens Falls shone above all the others. From 1867 to 1917, Stoddard produced hundreds of stereo cards, large-format "cabinet views," maps, guidebooks and, at the very end

of his career, picture postcards. Stoddard's way with words nearly matched his skill with a camera. His views and descriptions of the delights of Lake George and the greater Adirondacks may have contributed as much to the fame of the region as all other books and magazine articles combined.

As Stoddard's grip on the market loosened in the early 20th century, other talented pho-

The Narrows, winter detail, by John Henry Hill, 1871 (Adirondack Museum, Blue Mountain Lake)

tographers supplied the public appetite for images, among them Jesse S. Wooley of Ballston Spa who spent summers working at Silver Bay, and Fred Thatcher, who captured the gay life of Lake George in early decades of the 20th century.

Picture postcards only came on the scene in the early 20th century. Combining a pictorial souvenir with a postal message, the postcard became an instant hit. Early Lake George postcards capture the beginnings of cabin and motel-based vacations. At mid-century, another Glens Falls photographer rose to the challenge of capturing the local scenery on film. Dick Dean mastered the challenge of translating color photographs to four-color printing processes. His bright photographs of sparkling beaches, sky-blue water and carnival-colored theme parks continued the lively tradition of promoting Lake George for more than another half century.

Most artists came to Lake George for a summer sojourn to make sketches that they would turn into finished paintings in their studios. John Henry Hill came to stay – for four years. In the fall of 1870, he settled in for a solitary stay on Phantom Island. He sketched, painted, and produced a series of etchings on a press that he hauled across the ice from Bolton Landing.

Hotel Life

People traveled a long way to reach hotels on Lake George, so they settled in for a month or more once they arrived. Hotel spaces and activities had to be organized to keep people happily occupied even in bad weather. Guests mingled in the central dining rooms, gracious parlors and on the wide verandas facing the lake. The menu of activities served up each day appealed to Victorian taste for quiet recreation.

Hotel advertising boasted about fleets of rowboats or canoes, tennis or croquet courts, fish and game that could be caught nearby, and the occasional ride along a woodland bridle path. Proprietors also assured their guests that they wouldn't be deprived of essentials, like "city cooks," and "daily mail," which included current newspapers.

Group activities occupied the evenings. The Fort William Henry Hotel held a dance every Thursday night. Traveling entertainers, like

A MUSICAL AFTERNOON ON THE AIRY PORCH OF

Porch of the Hotel Marion, c. 1905 (Lake George Historical Association)

Steamboat *Minne-ha-ha*, retired at Black Mountain Point by S.R. Stoddard, 1880 (Hillview Free Library, Diamond Point)

Sagamore veranda, c. 1925 (William P. Gates collection)

"Sunflower Brigade" greeting guests at Hulett's Landing by H.A. Ogden, 1883 (Adirondack Museum, Blue Mountain Lake)

"Lollapalooza" the magician, made a seasonal circuit. Local musicians played both on land and on the water. Inevitably, employees also had to fill in, as in the case of the "Sunflower Brigade" that greeted the steamboat at Hulett's Landing, performing infantry drill with brooms in place of muskets, to the delight of onlookers.

Hotels hosted most of the visitors to Lake George during the latter half of the 19th century, when new urban jobs supported both the cost and the time for a family vacation. Working people did not fare so well. Mary Wiltsie Fuller of Troy, New York, wanted young women who worked in the shirt factories to have a summer vacation as well. With the financial help of Katrina and Spencer Trask and the organizational skills of Nellie Cluett, she founded Wiawaka Holiday House at East Lake George in 1903. The resort still offers rates adjusted to the resources of its guests.

The Sagamore Hotel has outlasted dozens of other Lake George establishments consumed by the very blazes that were meant to comfort their guests. First opened in 1883, the Sagamore rose from ashes in 1894 and again in 1933. Renovated for wintertime in the 1980s, today's Sagamore combines the gracious living of times past with the recreation options of the present day.

Intimate Communities

The heyday of hotel holidays began to wane in the early 20th century. Wooden hotel buildings caught fire easily. Proprietors came and went every few years. Young people who waited table, changed and laundered linens, and "smashed" baggage outgrew seasonal work. But the guests still wanted to return year after year.

Gradually, the organization of summer life changed. Families built their own places, expanding the hamlets surrounding the landings. At Glenburnie, and Rogers Rock, the hotels reorganized as clubs in the 1920s, providing rooms to members and serving as a social center for owners of surrounding cottages. Wealthy "cottagers" from Caldwell to Bolton Landing organized the Lake George Club as their social center.

Each main landing community developed its own unique personality. Caldwell (Lake George Village) was the center of activity, with the train and steamboat connections. Bolton Landing emerged as the artist's retreat. Hulett's Landing, Sabbath Day Point and Hague supported seasonal churches or a little library, architectural gems hidden away where one would least expect them.

David Smith's steel sculpture, *Voltron XVIII*, on his farm in Bolton, c. 1960 (Bolton Historical Museum, Bolton Landing)

The mansions of "Millionaire's Row" succumbed to the Great Depression and high taxes. Earl Woodward, the high school teacher from Ohio who had already made a fortune creating dude ranches out of abandoned logging camps in remote sections of Warren county, razed some of the mansions and divided the once-stately grounds into narrow strips for cottage colonies. From the 1940s through the 1960s, these cottage colonies were the most popular lodgings for Lake George visitors.

Grace Chapel at Sabbath Day Point by Gerald Abbott, c. 1970

Boathouse at Silver Bay, c. 1910 (Silver Bay Association, Hague)

Children's Summer Camps

Towards the end of the 19th century, progressive educators worried that the leisurely pace of resort life offered little to improve the physical or mental fitness of young people. They established summer camps devoted to active sports and wilderness skills that taught problem solving and self-reliance. Camps catered only to boys for several decades, but girls' camps were a part of the camping boom that followed World War I. The Adirondack Girl Scout Council opened their first camp, Wah-Ta-Wah in 1921 on a field adjacent to Rainbow Beach in Bolton.

Generations of campers recall singing around a council fire and learning Indian lore and crafts. These traditions came from the writings of a Canadian naturalist, Ernest Thompson Seton, who believed that the way to get

Silver Bay Association YMCA Conference and Training Center retains the essence of the Lake George experience in the oldest hotel on the lake, built in 1902. Each week a new contingent of conference groups come together to discuss faith, philosophy and to celebrate nature. They can rock on the broad veranda, paddle about in small boats and play games. Summer guests continue to share this comfortable fabric of community with retirees in surrounding cottages.

Girl Scouts at Camp Wah-Ta-Wah, c. 1921 (Girl Scouts of the Adirondack Council, Glens Falls)

Delaware Tent, Lake George Camp for Boys by George Phelps, 1922 (Crandall Library Center for Folklife, History and Cultural Programs, Glens Falls)

Boy Scouts of America held the very first Scout camp at Silver Bay in August 1910. At the Council Fire, attended by the British founder of Scouting, Robert Baden-Powel, Ernest Seton Thompson was named "Chief Scout." His book, *The Birch Bark Roll*, published in 1902 as the manual for the Woodcraft League, provided two-thirds of the content for the *Boy Scout Handbook*.

closer to Nature was to follow Indian ways. Many Adirondack camps still display their "Woodcraft League" certificate with Thompson's wolf print signature.

The Great Depression put many Adirondack camps out of business, but a camp revival after World War II helped drive the tourism boom of the 1950s. Families would bring their children to camp and rent a cottage or campsite nearby. Campers returned year after year, graduating to counselors, learning leadership skills and cementing an abiding love for Lake George.

Ernest Seton Thompson (far right) at the first American Boy Scout Camp, 1910 (Silver Bay Association, Hague)

"Free as Air"

So Seneca Ray Stoddard described a camp in the middle of Lake George in his *Book of Pictures of Lake George Islands* in 1910. By then, camping was an end in itself to spend time in the great outdoors, no longer the temporary bivouac of travelers, as when Francis Parkman stopped to wash out his breeches in 1842. A fishing club from Glens Falls called "The Waltonians" organized some of the earliest recreational camping in the 1850s. They named the island where they camped, north of Island Harbor in Hague, in honor of their namesake, the 17th-century author of *The Compleat Angler*.

Up until the 1920s, anyone could claim what Stoddard called "a lodge in the vast wilderness" by pitching camp. When private claims threatened public access, camping advocates lobbied hard for New York State owner-

Family camper c.1920 (Jim Charlton collection)

Glens Falls Waltonians by J.S. Crocker, 1870 (Crandall Library Center for Folklife, History and Cultural Programs, Glens Falls)

ship of the Lake George islands. Campers must now pay a nightly fee, but anyone who wants to can answer Stoddard's invitation to "Come up and dream."

Land around the lake was another matter. Early in the 20th century, families began to look for their own permanent place in the woods. Their camps often began as a wooden platform with a tent pitched over it. Crates of provisions, brought by steamboat, reinforced the sidewalls. Over time, solid structures replaced canvas. Even after guest, boat and pump houses had expanded the complex, a summer place was still called a "camp."

Fillmore's Camp, c. 1900 (Adirondack Museum, Blue Mountain Lake)

Fireplace in the gym at Silver Bay
by Elara Tanguy, 2005

Fayette Dunklee possessed the humble skill of stone masonry at just the right moment. He could assemble the random rocks available around Lake George into broad solid chimneys, perfectly suited to the rustic taste of summer people. Hague folks can point out several Dunklee chimneys in and around Silver Bay, including the grand fireplace in the gymnasium, built in 1917.

Passion for Watercraft

A sheet of water measuring almost forty-four square miles, Lake George has enticed every sort of boat enthusiast over the years. Racers of all kinds have sped across the broad expanses of open lake off Caldwell/Lake George Village, Bolton and Hague. Cozy passages between islands enticed anglers and lovers.

Early visitors hired small boats and oarsmen to row them to the islands, to favored fishing spots, or to make an expedition down the lake to visit the ruins of Fort Ticonderoga. Steam power replaced muscle as the tourism boom exploded. Small steam-powered launches carried pleasure parties into shallow coves where large boats could not go. They also ferried provisions and building material. Thirteen such craft plied the lake in 1880, fifty in 1892 and over a hundred at the turn of the 20th century.

The first meeting of the American Canoe Association on Canoe Island in Lake George in 1880 opened the era of personal watercraft on the lake. Annual regattas featured both paddling and sailing canoe races, enlivened by a "dump race" to climb back into an upset canoe. A procession of decorated launches, the high point of many regattas, gave spectators a way to participate in the competition.

Powerboats took Lake George by storm after the First World War, but sailing took a while longer. The National Champion Gold Cup Speedboat races followed their champions to Lake George on four occasions, first in 1914 and then three years in succession in the mid-1930s. That was also when Rogers Rock Yacht Club in Ticonderoga held the first regular sail-

American Canoe Association Regatta off Crosbyside, by S.R.
Stoddard,1882 (Chapman Historical Museum, Glens Falls)

Hydro-planing off Point Comfort, Pilot Knob, c. 1940. Sheila Reinhardsen in the boat (Private collection).

ing races. After World War II, sailing took off as the racing sport of choice. Since then, regular weekend races of Rainbows, Stars, Turnabouts, Comets, Flying Juniors, Optimists, and mixed-handicapped yachts have kept sailors of all ages on the water all summer long.

No one needs to own a boat to enjoy open water. Marinas in each community have boats to rent. Lake George Steamboat Company continues a long tradition of daily cruises from their docks on the waterfront in Lake George Village. The newest cruise boat, the *Adirondac,* was hauled overland from Lake Champlain in 2004.

The Lake George Steamboat Company has operated boats on Lake George almost continuously since 1817. For more than a century, steamboats served as the primary link between lakeshore hamlets and hotels. After World War II, Wilbur Dow, a New York City Admiralty lawyer, revived the company for tourist excursions. Today, thousands of visitors a year discover the "Queen of American Lakes" from the decks of the *Mohican, Lac du Saint Sarement* or *Minne-Ha-Ha.*

Lake George Regatta Association program, 1912 (Lake George Historical Association)

Keeping Entertained

Visitors to Lake George needed more than boating and fishing to keep them busy for days on end. As time went by, the gentle court sports lost their luster. Lake George resorts have had to reinvent themselves every generation in order to keep their guests happy.

The drama of history proved a draw from the beginning. Thomas Jefferson (1791), Abby May (1800) and Benjamin Silliman (1820) thrilled to the stories of the Marquis de Mont-

Steamboat *Mohican* towing skiers, c. 1965 (*Lake George Mirror* collection)

Prospect Mountain Cable Incline Railway, c. 1900 (Lake George Historical Association)

calm's siege of Fort William Henry, General Abercromby's terrible defeat at Fort Carillon and Henry Knox's heroic effort to haul artillery across the ice from that "old French Fort," Ticonderoga. Nineteenth-century guidebooks retold every one of these stories. In the twentieth century, restorations of Fort Ticonderoga (1909) and Fort William Henry (1953) brought them to life.

Getting high up on a mountain remains a perennial pleasure, but only Prospect Mountain offers an alternative to climbing. The first Prospect Mountain House Hotel (1877) was accessible by carriage road. Twenty years later, a cog railway opened, running straight up from the village of Lake George. Unfortunately, riders supported it for only eight years. The tourist boom of the 1950s triggered State interest in

Bella Vista Casino by Fred Thatcher, c. 1920 (Lake George Historical Association)

building Prospect Mountain Veterans Memorial Highway, which opened in 1969.

Nightlife continued around the lake even after hotels gave way to cottage communities. Summer folks had their pick of casinos and dance halls in Lake George, Hulett's Landing and Gull Bay. Young people didn't need to worry about driving mountain roads in the dark if they had access to a boat. Dancing may now be out of style, but music still floats across the water from Lake George Village.

Vacation fun changed dramatically after World War II, when veterans took to the road with their young families. Lake George responded with a host of new attractions. Million Dollar Beach made a priceless view available to everyone in 1951. In 1954, Charles Wood designed "Storytown" as a place for families to play together, based on a Mother Goose fairy-tale theme. His "theme park" idea spread throughout the region. Soon, families could choose from Animal Land, Floating Rock, Magic Forest or Time Town along Route 9.

For two hundred years, the rough terrain of ruined bastions and trenches presented enough of an obstacle to construction that the site of Fort William Henry remained undisturbed. When the tourist boom following World War II threatened to obliterate the remains, a consortium of local businessmen undertook excavation and reconstruction of the fort beginning in 1953. Two years later, a restoration of Fort William Henry opened to the public.

Storytown by Richard K. Dean, c. 1955

Cannon embrasure at Fort William Henry (Fort William Henry, Lake George Village)

"Charley" Wood wrote a new chapter in vacation entertainment when he opened "Storytown" in 1954. His park followed the "theme" of Mother Goose stories before anyone had ever heard of a theme park. Wood added to his magic with the "Gay 90s" Gas Light Village in 1959 and ultimately transformed his first success into The Great Escape. He also gave back to his community, in support of The Hyde Collection, Double "H" Hole in the Woods Camp and the Glens Falls Hospital cancer wing.

Kayaking on Dunham Bay marsh, 2004 (Lake George Land Conservancy, Bolton Landing)

It took the Great Depression to generate proactive work. President Franklin D. Roosevelt's Emergency Conservation Work Act of 1933 called for a Civilian Conservation Corps that would put young, unemployed men to work planting trees. Several Corps went to work within the Lake George watershed. Today, the many acres of Warren County forest planted by members of the CCC can be seen across from the County Municipal Center and on the road over Tongue Mountain.

New York State created the Lake George Park Commission in 1961 and expanded its authority in 1988. The commissioners, almost all of whom are residents of lakeshore communities, oversee the details of lake recreation, from dock permits and boat registration to marine patrol. The Commission also takes responsibil-

Caring for Land and Water

Not many years went by before people began to realize that Lake George could be loved too much. The hotel era was just dawning when William H.H. "Adirondack" Murray wrote *Adventures in the Wilderness* (1869), a book that would unleash an avalanche of tourists. At the same time, stocks of fish and game animals were already in such decline that the New York State legislature began to implement wildlife protection laws.

Private initiative picked up the cause, as the Lake George Association came together to regulate fishing in 1885. They soon turned their attention to trying to persuade industries in Ticonderoga to stop manipulating the flow of

water over the dam at the outlet. By the end of the next century, the Association had published a citizen's guide to water quality that demonstrated how to use the tools of military siege craft – gabions and fascines – to buttress the landscape against erosion. A "Floating Classroom" out on the water coordinates with a land component at Up Yonda Farm in Bolton.

Naturalists targeted timber cutting as the reason for a decline in sport fish and water quality as early as the 1850s. Conservation efforts established the New York State Forest Preserve in 1885, then the Adirondack Park in 1892, following up two years later with a constitutional amendment to keep State land "forever wild."

John Apperson's winter camp at Bolton Historical Museum by Elara Tanguy, 2005

ity for implementing storm water regulations and control of invasive species like Urasian milfoil and zebra mussels.

By the end of the 20th century, development pressures threatened large tracts of open space that remained relatively untouched by human activity. A new generation of conservation organizations found fresh ways to protect the landscape and water quality of Lake George. The FUND for Lake George raises support for programs and organizations dedicated to protecting the lake. The Lake George Land Conservancy works to protect natural places for future generations while the Darrin Fresh Water Institute applies the latest scientific knowledge to combat the biological enemies that assault the Lake George environment.

The chronicle of these caretakers of the lake can be read in the pages of the *Lake George Mirror,* which reports their victories over a multitude of threats to the lake every week during the summer season and monthly during the winter.

John Apperson loved camping on Lake George so much that he even came in winter. He designed a hand-held sail that propelled him across the ice. He and his buddies from General Electric in Schenectady didn't want to lose their favorite get-aways, so they organized a conservation movement to add the Lake George islands to the New York State Forest Preserve.

Civilian Conservation Corps forest, Tongue Mountain by Elara Tanguy, 2005

Town-by-Town Gazetteer

Hague

Two of the most dramatic cliffs on Lake George bracket the Town of Hague. Deer Leap on Tongue Mountain marks the southern boundary; Rogers Rock the north. In between, mountains rise steeply from the lake, leaving only a few patches of gently sloping ground.

A series of hamlets occupy these footholds. Furthest south is Sabbath Day Point, which Theodore Dwight described in his guidebook, *The Northern Traveler* (1825) as offering one of the three best views on Lake George. Further north, Silver Bay is home to the Silver Bay Association YMCA Conference and Training Center whose substantial hotel dates back to the turn of the 20th century. The hamlet of Hague sits on the meager delta formed by Hague Brook, whose course offered the best route for a road to bring ore down from the graphite mines in the western part of town.

Since the mines closed in 1921, Hague has concentrated on welcoming summer vacationers. The first farmhouse inns gave way to substantial hotels and finally to motels and summer cottages. The broad expanse of Lake George's North Basin has plenty of room for boat races, which started in 1880 with the Hague Rowing Club, and continue with the Northern Lake George Yacht Club's sailing regattas. Summer visitors fill the air with the sound of water sport. Winter visitors are a quiet lot, for they are thousands of sleeping bats, cozy in their hibernaculum in the old graphite mines.

Henry Shattuck at Catamount Club hunting camp, c. 1900 (West Historical Museum, Hague)

Lake George "monster" by Elara Tanguy, 2005

Harry Watrous earned his legendary status by playing the greatest practical joke in Hague history. Watrous fashioned a "Lake George Monster," which he made to swim across Island Harbor by means of ropes and pulleys. He timed the monster's "attack" to startle passing boaters. "Georgie" is on display in the Hague Community Center.

HAGUE TOWN HALL (518) 543-6161

Museums and Sites of Interest

West Historical Museum

Silver Bay Association YMCA Conference and Training Center

Indian Kettles

Public Water Frontage

Hague beach and boat launch

Rogers Rock State Campground

Recreation

Deer Leap & Tongue Mountain Trails

Jabe Pond Trail

Rogers Rock Trail

Spruce Mountain Trail

Ticonderoga Country Club

Indian Kettles, c. 1920 (West Historical Museum, Hague)

Bolton

Bolton embraces dramatic mountains and the largest stretch of open water in Lake George. The shores of Northwest Bay once lay at the upper reaches of a watershed before Ice Age glaciers gouged out the Lake George Narrows to the north, molding the terrain to its present form. Early settlers practiced subsistence farming, but later the local harvest of trees moved quickly through the mills of Sawmill Bay.

Summer travelers began to arrive shortly after the Civil War, generating a whole new business based on the natural beauty of the lake and mountains. Steamboats made regular stops at hotels on the larger islands and at the main dock at Bolton Landing. Prosperous families built grand houses by the lake and enjoyed the company of famous artists who found a peaceful haven here.

A blend of aesthetic and physical pleasures generated conscious appreciation for the natural environment and concern for its welfare. Even before the days when the Civilian Conservation Corps ("CCC") planted hundreds of acres of trees on Tongue Mountain and surrounding State lands, Bolton harbored conservationist sentiments and activists. John Apperson spearheaded the movement to protect the Lake George Islands in the early 20th century. At the other end of the century, Darrin

David Smith working on *Tanktotem IX* in his studio at Bolton, 1960 (Art © estate of David Smith licensed by VAGA, New York, NY)

Fresh Water institute brought the scientific expertise of Rensselaer Polytechnic Institute to bear on the growing "invisible" challenge of how to preserve Lake George water quality while the Lake George Land Conservancy went to work protecting open space around the lake.

David Smith purchased a place in Bolton in 1929, just a year after his first visit. Unlike other famous artists who came only for the summer, Smith made this his permanent home once REA brought electricity to his hill farm in 1940. He filled the fields with extraordinary metal sculptures that were dispersed to major museums after his death in 1965.

Cat Mountain from a Point Opposite Bolton by David Johnson, 1873 (Adirondack Museum, Blue Mountain Lake)

Museums and Sites of Interest
- Bolton Free Library
- Bolton Historical Museum
- Darrin Fresh Water Institute
- Lake George Land Conservancy
- Marcella Sembrich Opera Museum
- Sagamore Hotel
- Up Yonda Farm

Public Water Frontage
- Northwest Bay car-top boat launch
- Rogers Park Beach
- Veteran's Park Beach
- Lake George Islands State Campground

Recreation
- Cat and Thomas Mountains Preserve
- Clay Meadows Trail to Five Mile Point & Tongue Mountain
- Municipal Tennis Courts
- Pole Hill Pond Trail
- Sagamore Golf Course

Transportation
- Lake George Shoreline Cruises
- Lake George Steamboat Company cruises
- Greater Glens Falls Transit System

Speedboat racing mogul George Reis tuning *El Lagarto* for the Gold Cup races, 1935 (Bolton Historian)

Lake George

The gateway to Lake George from the south witnessed a wilderness battle, a devastating siege and many military campaign seasons a generation before the American Revolution. After the war, General James Caldwell parlayed his land patent into a thriving community spread across the high ground where the French General Montcalm had placed his cannon batteries in 1757, with a full complement of mills strung along English Brook.

The sandy beach where British forces launched their bateaux to attack New France soon experienced a more peaceful invasion. Travelers making the switch from stagecoach to steamboat at Caldwell fell in love with the stunning view down the lake. Some wrote about the scenery while others sketched and painted the dramatic prospect. By the middle of the 19th century, Caldwell had become a destination in itself. Grand hotels catered to guests who came for months at a time and needed a fleet of small craft to keep them entertained.

Vacation styles changed dramatically by the middle of the 20th century, when Americans put the Great Depression and a world war behind them and embraced the family vacation. Caldwell changed its style in response, even changing its name to Lake George. Theme parks catering to children added to the mix of sporting diversions in and around Battlefield Park, where sculptures and monuments commemorate historical figures as far back as Father Isaac Jogues, who gave the lake its first European name, Lac du Saint Sacrement, in 1646. These days, young people – and the young at heart — flock to Million Dollar Beach and the Lake Front Walkway to enjoy the bustling activity in a place affectionately called "The Village."

The Marquis de Montcalm brought an army of 8,000 soldiers and 1800 Indians to lay siege to Fort William Henry in August of 1757 in an effort to retain control of the lake the French called Lac du Saint Sacrement. Distortions of the story began with contemporary press reports and continued into literature, as James Fenimore Cooper made the battle famous in his novel, *Last of the Mohicans*, published in 1826.

Chamber of Commerce (518) 668-5755

Museums and Historic Sites
    Fort William Henry
    Lake George Battlefield Park
    Lake George Historical Association
    Lake George Village Visitor Center
    Prospect Mountain Veterans Memorial
        Highway
    Sacred Heart Church's Father Jogues
        windows
Public Water Frontage
    Lake Avenue Park & car-top boat launch
    Lake Front Walkway
    Million Dollar Beach
    Shepard Park & Village Beach
    Usher Park & tennis courts

Garwood Speedboat dock, c. 1955 (Lake George Historian)

Motorcyclists at railroad station, c. 1935 (Lake George Village Historian)

Recreation
- Hearthstone Point Campground
- Lake George Battleground Campground
- Lake George Recreation Center & Forum
- Prospect Mountain Trail
- Warren County Bicycle Trail

Transportation
- Adirondack Trailways Bus
- Greater Glens Falls Transit System
- Greyhound Bus Lines
- Lake George Shoreline Cruises
- Lake George Steamboat Company

Aerial view of Lake George lakefront, c. 1960 (Fort William Henry, Lake George Village)

Queensbury

Queensbury spans the territory between the Hudson River and Lake George. During the colonial wars, British armies built their military road along an ancient Indian pathway connecting the two waterways. In 1755, a sequence of three engagements known collectively as the Battle of Lake George unfolded along this route.

Quakers established Queensbury in 1762, soon after the French and Indian War ended. Fifteen years later, Burgoyne's British campaign against the American rebellion drove them back to their native Dutchess County. The Revolutionary War interrupted settlement only briefly. Good farmland in the eastern valleys soon fed the needs of several mill hamlets. The largest of these grew into first the village (1839) and then the city of Glens Falls (1908).

Queensbury's link between the river and the lake offered new opportunities as the township center grew. Summer cottages began to appear on the shores of Assembly Point, around Cleverdale and at Joshua Rock at the end of the 19th century, creating convenient holiday retreats at the north end of town. Theme parks aimed at visitors to Lake George sprang up along Route 9. Open space filled rapidly with suburban housing and shopping centers during the boom years following the Second World War. A modern suburban community thrives today.

Edward Eggleston evolved from minister to journalist to novelist before settling on writing history, which he believed should record the culture of a people rather than politics and war. He delivered lectures around the country in winter and returned to Owl's Nest, his home at Joshua Rock on Dunham Bay to write. In 1894, Eggleston established Mountainside Free Library, which still operates like an old-fashioned library society.

Brown's Half-way House by S.R. Stoddard, 1880 (Caldwell-Lake George Library, Lake George Village)

Mountainside Free Library
by Elara Tanguy, 2005

WARREN COUNTY TOURISM DEPARTMENT
(800) 365-1050

Museums and Historic Sites
　Williams Monument
Public Water Frontage
　Glen Lake Road Launch Site
　Feeder Canal
　Hudson River Boat Launch

Recreation
　Bay Meadows Golf Course
　Gurney Lane Recreation Park
　Hiland Golf Course
　Queensbury Country Club
　Sunnyside Golf Course
　Top O' the World Golf Course
　Warren County Bicycle Trail
　West Mountain Ski area

Transportation
　Adirondack Trailways Bus
　Floyd Bennett Memorial Airport (noncommercial)
　Greyhound Bus
　Greater Glens Falls Transit System

American Canoe Association Regatta by S.R. Stoddard, 1882 (Hillview Free Library, Diamond Point)

Glens Falls

Glens Falls grew quickly around the power source first known as "Wing's Falls" on the Hudson River. Sawmills dominated the riverfront from the beginning, turning timber from the foothills of the Adirondacks into lumber. Managing logs in the river proved a difficult challenge until mill owners organized a "Big Boom" at the "Big Bend" above Glens Falls to sort and store the thousands of logs moving down river to the mills. Local limestone deposits supplied black marble and raw material for the "Jointa Lime" and Portland Cement companies, still an important part of the local

Under the Arch at Glens Falls by S.R. Stoddard, c.1880 (Chapman Historical Museum, Glens Falls)

Self Portrait by Seneca Ray Stoddard, c.1880 (Chapman Historical Museum, Glens Falls)

economy. The Feeder and Champlain Canals and later the railroads provided a transportation link to the nation. Supported by paper and cotton mills, shirt and collar factories and insurance and finance companies, the bustling village grew into a regional commercial center that officially achieved city status in 1908.

Photography set Glens Falls apart from most river mill towns. Two local talents, working a century apart, capitalized on the aura of Lake George and the nearby Adirondacks to build businesses that dominated their markets. Seneca Ray Stoddard supplied the early tourist trade with stereo views, guidebooks, maps, and high quality prints of popular destinations and vistas. In the mid 20th century, Dick Dean propelled a new wave of tourism with inviting full color photographs and postcards of the region's attractions and scenery.

James Fenimore Cooper captivated early American readers with thrilling stories about their historical past. In *Last of the Mohicans*, published in 1826, Cooper wove a saga of war in the wilderness that cast Lake George as "Horicon." Supposedly inspired by a visit to Glens Falls, Cooper brought his drama to its climax in a cave under the waterfall. "Cooper's Cave" has fascinated visitors ever since.

Downtown Glens Falls, c. 1895 (Chapman Historical Museum, Glens Falls)

Today, Glens Falls enjoys a wide range of civic activities and cultural organizations. Art and history museums offer cultural opportunities typical of a much larger city. The Crandall Public Library reaches beyond information access to maintain an extensive historical archive and Folklife Center. Theatre and musical performances, sports events and even rodeos attract audiences from a largely rural region.

Lake George's Eastern Shore

Three small hamlets cluster about the places where shelter for boat landings coincided with overland access to the Champlain Valley and the railroad.

Hulett's Landing lies opposite the northern end of Tongue Mountain, and five miles from the "Chubb's Dock" station in Dresden. Seneca Ray Stoddard's 1875 guide to Lake George called it "the wildest" as well as one of the oldest settlements on the lake. After Philander Hulett started taking in summer boarders at his farm in about 1870, new owners expanded to accommodate fifty and then a hundred guests, adding a covered walkway, summerhouse and reflecting pool. By the end of the century, entertainments included a music hall and a fleet of Saint Lawrence skiffs. Ten years later, new Rushton canoes had been added to the boat and canoe livery. Eventually, interest in private cottages overcame the fashion for hotel holidays.

Gull Bay in the town of Putnam emerged along with the twentieth-century interest in camp life. Camp Wah-Na-Gi for girls operated on Smith's Bay from 1910 to 1934. The craggy overlook called Glen Eyrie lured hikers and family campers. There were only a handful of rustic camps until after World War II when the large holdings were divided up into lakeside lots.

Shear family camping at Glen Eyrie, c.1920 (Jim Charlton collection)

Glenburnie surrounds Blaire's Bay, sheltered from the north wind by Anthony's Nose across the lake from Hague. This comfortable old summer colony sprang from the outdoor enthusiasm of Ernest Walton who, as a college student, convinced his father to buy up the Blaire's Bay Farm. With engineering degree in hand, Walton surveyed the site, then designed and built a hotel that opened in 1909. He designed and built cottages for many family members. Glenburnie became a club in 1927, thereby getting out of the hotel business. Camp Adirondack on the isolated point to the south celebrated its centennial in 2004.

Guarding the pinched passage of the lake's outlet to the north, Black Point bears witness to one of Ticonderoga's early landowners. Prince Taylor, a "Free Black," developed a prosperous farm where he employed a several indentured servants. Thomas Jefferson and James Madison found this remarkable when they visited in the spring of 1791.

George Knapp bought 9500 acres and nearly ten miles of shoreline south of Hulett's Landing in 1894. As founder of Union Carbide, he probably introduced carbide-gas plants to the local hotels. His rustic mansion clung to cliffs of Shelving Rock Mountain from 1902–1914. Most of the Knapp Estate became part of the New York State Forest Preserve in 1941.

Hulett's Landing by S.R. Stoddard, 1880 (Chapman Historical Museum, Glens Falls)

Gull Bay Preserve, 2004 (Lake George Land Conservancy, Bolton Landing)

Neighboring Regions

First Wilderness

Communities along the Hudson River, upstream from Glens Falls and west of Lake George, have joined together to celebrate their shared history along the earliest route into the heart of the Adirondack wilderness.

From the Great Falls of the Hudson, upriver to the dramatic Hudson River Gorge, the stream tumbles over falls and rapids, past dramatic cliffs of magnificent marble impregnated with sharp chunks of gneiss, then slows to flow easily through ice meadows, kept perpetually open by the annual scouring of spring ice floes.

A series of falls and incoming tributaries made ideal town sites. Corinth straddles the short stretch between the Great Falls of the Hudson and Palmer's Falls. Hadley and Lake Luzerne flank the confluence of the Great Sacandaga River. Warrensburg sits astride the Schroon River just east of where it joins the Hudson at Thurman Station. North Creek marks the historic terminus of the Adirondack Railroad Company at the foot of Gore Mountain. In between, the crossroads hamlets of Stony Creek, The Glen and Riparius carry on a tradition of wilderness recreation dating back to the mid 19th century.

The "First Wilderness Corridor" served as a hunting ground for Indian people, who established trails connecting the Mohawk Valley with the Champlain Valley. Soldiers followed

A Jam at Luzerne by S. R. Stoddard, c. 1880 (Chapman Historical Museum, Glens Falls)

The Glen on the Hudson River by S. R. Stoddard, c. 1880 (Chapman Historical Museum, Glens Falls)

these trails during the French and Indian War. Once fighting had subsided, the vast tracts of timber beckoned. Logging and tanning held sway even as Americans discovered the lure of a vanishing wilderness. Construction of a railroad just after the Civil War gave vacationers easy access to hotels and resorts. Today, the scenic Upper Hudson River Railroad runs on the old tracks during the summer season.

Champlain Canal Region
The "Lake George Loop" of Lakes to Locks Passage meets the Champlain Canal Region at Hudson Falls, where early travelers on the Hudson River had to unload their gear and travel overland to either Lake George or Lake Champlain before continuing a northward journey. America's war for independence was

Delaware and Hudson Railroad Depot, Fort Edward, c. 1910 (Old Fort House, Fort Edward)

Lock on the Champlain Canal, 1895 (Fort Ticonderoga)

not yet over when General Philip Schuyler suggested that a canal could be built along the portage route to Lake Champlain. His dream became reality following the War of 1812.

The Champlain Canal began carrying cargo on the northern leg between Fort Edward and Whitehall in 1819. It reached south to Waterford where it intersected the Erie Canal in 1823. The main streets of every town along the canal's 64 mile course reflect the prosperity brought by cheap transportation. An expanded barge canal built in the early years of the 20th century followed the Hudson River channel, so remains of the early canal tow path, locks and viaducts can be still be found in the landscape.

Today, the Champlain Canal route offers great recreation opportunities. Cycling and walking trails follow the level course of the old towpath while boaters can spend a day on the canal or lock through to Lake Champlain on an international voyage to the Richelieu River of Quebec. History buffs can explore antique shops, colonial forts and the turning point of the Revolutionary War. A regional map brochure and companion guidebook help visitors find the way to the many sites and features of the Champlain Canal region.